THE SECOND BOOK OF SOPRANO SOLOS

PART II

compiled by Joan Frey Boytim

G. SCHIRMER, Inc.

DISTRIBUTED BY

HAL•LEONARD®
CORPORATION
7777 W. BLUEMOUND RD. P.O. BOX 13819 MILWAUKEE, WI 53213

PREFACE

Many teachers have expressed the desire to have a second volume to complement *The Second Book of Solos* series for those high school and college students studying more advanced student literature. In my studio, I have found that students using the four volumes of *Easy Songs for Beginning Singers* in seventh and eighth grades move very easily into *The First Book of Solos* and *The First Book of Solos–Part II* in ninth and tenth grades. Several of my students have moved into *The Second Book of Solos* as early as eleventh grade. They would find the variety of *The Second Book of Solos–Part II* a welcome addition to their repertoire for eleventh and twelfth grades. With many of today's college freshmen using *The First Book of Solos* and *The First Book of Solos–Part II*, *The Second Book of Solos* and this new *Part II* will prove to be a great launching pad of further new repertoire for freshman and sophomores.

The songs introduced in this volume are on comparable levels of sophistication and musical difficulty with those found in *The Second Book of Solos*, and could be used at the same time to provide more variety of repertoire. Each voice volume has representative English, American, Russian, Italian, German, French, sacred, oratorio, and Gilbert and Sullivan selections not used previously in any of my other anthologies. There are a number of out-of-print songs which deserved to be reissued, and quite a number of unfamiliar songs which should find a place in student repertoire.

In these volumes we have been able to include pieces from more contemporary composers such as Barber, Bax, Bowles, Chanler, Duke, Dougherty, Hoiby, Ives, Griffes, Gurney, Lekberg, Sacco, Thomson, and Warlock. The relatively unknown French composer, Félix Fourdrain, is represented in three of the four volumes. These songs, as well as other unfamiliar French mélodies, have only been available in single sheet form and have never before had English singing translations. For these songs, a life-long vocal accompanist and retired French professor, Harry Goldby, has made very singable texts which relate very closely to the original poems. My excitement mounts when I think of those students who will enjoy learning many of these more unfamiliar songs, as well as those songs that have been difficult to find.

This set of four books will conclude the more advanced portion of this 16 volume basic series of teaching material for soprano, mezzo-soprano/alto, tenor, and baritone/bass (the four volumes of *The First Book of Solos*, the four volumes of *The First Book of Solos–Part II*, the four volumes of *The Second Book of Solos*, and now the four volumes of *The Second Book of Solos–Part II*). There are 528 different songs included in the 16 volumes, with an average of 132 songs of all varieties carefully chosen for content and suitability for each voice part. I only wish I had had all of these books for teaching when my studio began over 45 years ago!

Joan Frey Boytim
May, 2004

CONTENTS

ALLELUJA

from *Exsultate, Jubilate*

Wolfgang Amadeus Mozart
(1756-1791)

5

* The accidental is a variant which appears in some editions.

al - le - lu - ja.

Al - le - lu - ja, al - le - lu - ja,

al - le - lu - ja, al - le - lu - ja,

al - le - lu -

8

* The lower note is a variant which appears in some editions.

ALS LUISE DIE BRIEFE IHRES UNGETREUEN
(Louise Burns Her Love Letters)

Gabriele von Baumberg
English version by Lorraine Noel Finley

Wolfgang Amadeus Mozart
(1756-1791)

Ihr dan - ket Flam - - men eu - er
You owe ex - ist - ence to a

Sein: ich geb' euch nun den Flam - men
fire, So to a fire I now re -

wie - der, und all die schwär - me - ri - schen
turn you; And you, his ar - dent songs, I

Lie - der, denn_ ach!— er sang nicht mir al -
burn you, For_ I was not his sole de -

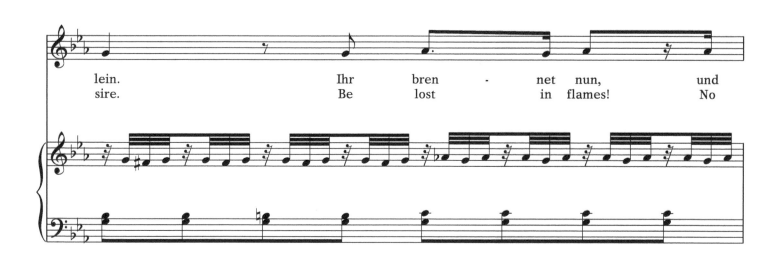

lein. Ihr bren - net nun, und
sire. Be lost in flames! No

bald, ihr Lie - ben, ist kei - ne
more you'll taunt me, And of your

APRÈS UN RÊVE
(After a Dream)

Romain Bussine
English version by Theodore Baker

Gabriel Fauré
(1845-1924)

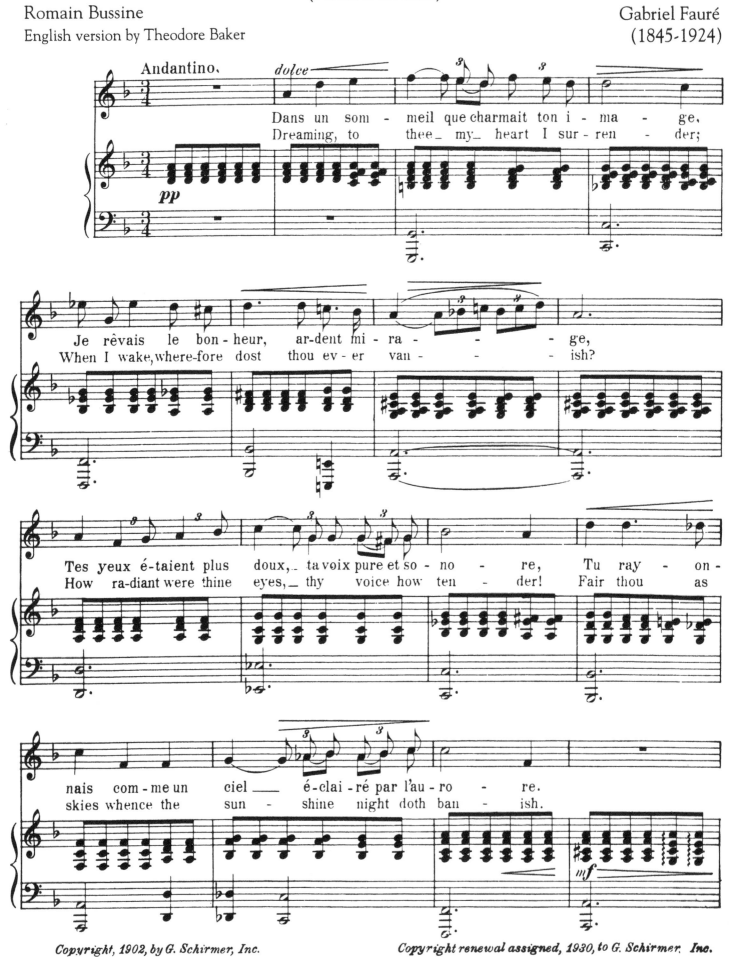

Dans un som - meil que charmait ton i - ma - ge,
Dreaming, to thee my heart I sur - ren - der;

Je rêvais le bon - heur, ar-dent mi - ra - - ge,
When I wake, where-fore dost thou ev - er van - - ish?

Tes yeux é-taient plus doux, ta voix pure et so - no - re, Tu ray - on -
How ra-diant were thine eyes, thy voice how ten - der! Fair thou as

nais com - me un ciel é-clai - ré par l'au - ro - re.
skies whence the sun - shine night doth ban - ish.

son - - - ges, Je t'ap-pel - le, ô nuit,___ rends-moi tes men-
tice ___ me, Should I a - gain___ in thy love re-

son - - ges, Re - viens, re - viens ra-di-
joice ___ me! Be mine, be mine for___

eu - - se, Re - viens, ô nuit mys-té-ri-
ev - - er, Re - turn, oh love, un-to thy

eu - - - - - se!
lov - - - - - er!

LA BELLE AU BOIS DORMANT
(Sleeping Beauty)

André Alexandre
English version by Harry Goldby

Félix Fourdrain
(1880-1923)

en cédant

Elle a - per - çut à son che - vet Ses cour - ti - sans,
She then per - ceived right by her side Her cour - te - sans,

suivez

ses cré - a - tu - res, Et d'un pe - tit geste in - qui - et Se blot - tit sous
real - ly her ser - vants, With a ges - ture show - ing dis - dain. She then snug - gled

p

a tempo

les cou - ver - tu - res.
back in her cush - ions of silk.

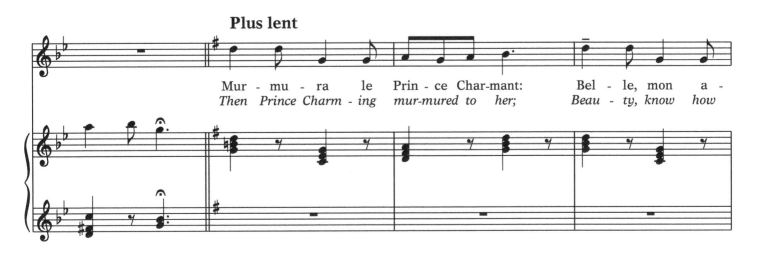

Plus lent

Mur - mu - ra le Prin - ce Char-mant: Bel - le, mon a -
Then Prince Charm - ing mur-mured to her; Beau - ty, know how

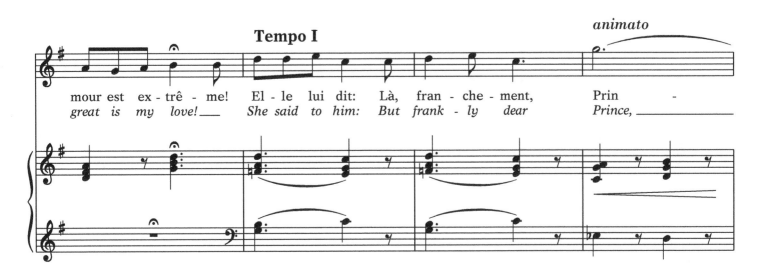

Tempo I

animato

mour est ex - trê - me! El - le lui dit: Là, fran - che - ment, Prin -
great is my love!___ She said to him: But frank - ly dear Prince,___

rall.

a tempo

- ce, il est u - sé vo - tre the - me.
you're out of date with a line like that.

Moins vite

Veuil - lez donc pour cent ans en - cor Re - tour - ner dans vo - tre pro - vin - ce;
Go a - way for one hun - dred years Back to cast - les where you be - long;

retenez   **rit.**

Je rê - vais d'oi - seaux, de fleurs d'or Et vous me de - ran - gez, cher prin - ce!
I was dream - ing of gol - den flow'rs And you've bro - ken the spell, dear prince!

Tempo I (scherzando)

p

Ain - si la bel - le s'ex - pli - qua De - vant u - ne cour stu - pé - fai - te,
And so dear beau - ty pled her case Look - ing at her stup - i - fied court,

Moins vite en cédant

opt.

Et tous lui re - pro - chaient dé - jà Ce grave ou - bli de l'é - ti - quet - te,
They all re - proached her quite up - set: This griev - ous breach of e - ti - quette,

to Bidú Sayão

THE BIRD

Elinor Wylie*

John Duke
(1899-1984)

O clear and mu-si-cal, Sing a-gain! Sing a-gain!

Hear the rain fall Through the long night,

CARE SELVE
(Lovely woodland)
from *Atalanta*

George Frideric Handel
(1685-1759)

English version by Shibley Boyes

trac - cia del mio cor, ven - go in trac - cia del mio cor,_____
yearn - ing, I come, come in quest _ of my true love,_____

_____ del mio _ cor, ven - go in trac - cia
_____ my true _ love, in ___ quest _____ of

del ___ mio cor.
my ___ true love.

CHANSON NORVÉGIENNE
(A Norwegian Song)

André Alexandre
English version by Harry Goldby

Félix Fourdrain
(1880-1923)

Allegro moderato ♩ = 108

Je - suis pri - se d'u - ne tris - tes - se
O - ver - come with dis - tress and sad - ness

Qui pè - sè, pè - se lour - de - ment:
Which heav - i - ly weighs on my heart;

Il me tra - hit, il me dé - lais - se,
He be - trays me, he leaves me hope - less,

Ce - lui que j'ai - me ten - dre - ment.
He whom I love so ten - der - ly.

C'est fête au vil - lage et je dan - se,
It's the vil - lage fair and I'm danc - ing,

Pour ca - cher ma dou - leur, _____
To con - ceal my great pain, _____

hé - las!   Mais il me sem - ble, á cha - que pas,   En -
A - las!   *But how it seems, at ev - 'ry step,*   *I*

ten - dre cri - er ma souf - fran - ce!
hear all the cries of my suf - fer - ing!

Au - des - sus _____ des fiords de Nor -
Far a - bove _____ the fiords of __

lar - mes, Et la dan - se n'ar - rê - te
plead - ing, *While* *the* *danc - ing* *stops* *not* *at*

pas,
all.

Mais il me sem - ble, à cha-que pas, Tour - no - yer
To me it seems, __ at ev - 'ry step, I am swirl -

CLAVELITOS
(Carnations)

Joaquín Valverde
(1846-1910)

English version by Mrs. M. T. E. Sandwith

sen - cia, pre - sen - cia y po - ten - cia que usté ve - ra en mi!
die, For her heart was mine own And her love mine a - lone!

ten.

Cla - ve -
White car -

colla voce

a tempo

li - tos _____
na - tions! _____

a tempo

ten.

Que los trai - go bo - ni - tos _____ pa mi
Fair and pure as my true __ love! _____ *Red car -*

colla voce

no - vio _____ los trai - go re - ven - to - nes chi - pé!
na - tions! _____ Like the red of her lips when she smiled,

Por - que tie - ne mu - chis - mo quin - qué, pa ro - bar co - ra -
When the flush of her beau - ty be - guiled, Rous - ing pas - sions un -

zo - nes o - lé! Y en - se - ñar - tes la e - sen - cia, pre - sen - cia y po -
ho - ly and wild; But her lips, false and red, Told a love quick - ly

ten - cia que ya sa - be us - té! Si tu me quie - res mi
sped, All too soon cold and dead! Mad - ly your per - fume stirs

Yo te quie-ro más a ti mi ca - ni, y to-dos los cla-ve-
heart still is true, Beat-ing on-ly for you! Come to me, love, ere the

li - tos bo - ni - tos, ___ to-dos se - rán pa - ra ti!
day-light shall see, Come, O queen of my heart, come to me!

To - dos son pa - ra ti, pa - ra ti, pa - ra ti, pa - ra
Come, O queen of my heart! Come, O queen of my heart, come to

ti! _____
me! _____

DOMINE DEUS
from *Gloria*

Antonio Vivaldi
(1678-1743)

Largo

Do - mi - ne De - us, Rex cœ - le -
O _____ Lord al - migh - ty, King of Heav -

stis, De - us Pa - ter, De - us
en, God _____ the Fa - ther, God _____ the

Pa - - - - - - ter _____ om - ni - po -
Fa - - - - - - ther _____ om - ni - po -

tens. Do -
tent. O _____

[mf]

tr

tr

[p]

De - us, Do - mi - ne De - us, Rex cœ - le - stis,
migh - ty, Lord _____ al - migh - ty, King of Heav - en,

De - us Pa - ter, De - us Pa - ter, Pa -
God the Fa - ther, God the Fa - ther, Fa -

[mf]

- - - - ter, Pa -
- - - - ther, the

[p]

mf

ter __ om - ni - po - tens, Pa -
Fa - ther om - ni - po - tent, God _____ the

CRABBED AGE AND YOUTH

William Shakespeare

C. Hubert H. Parry
(1848-1918)

Capriccioso

Crab - bed Age and Youth Can-not live to-ge-ther: Youth is full of plea - sance,

Age is full of care, Youth like sum-mer morn, Age like win-ter weath-er,

Youth like sum-mer brave, Age like win - ter bare:

poco rit.   *f a tempo*

Age _____ I do ab - hor _ thee,

f

poco rit.

Youth _____ I do a - dore _ thee; O my Love _ my Love, _ is

sf

a tempo   *f*

young!   Age _____ I do de -

f

opt.

fy   thee.

ff   *p*

Meno mosso

O sweet shep - herd, _ hie _ thee, For me-thinks, for me-

thinks, for me - thinks _ thou _ stay'st for me-thinks thou

poco rit.　　　　　　　　　　a tempo

stay'st ＿＿＿＿＿＿＿＿＿＿＿ too long.

THE FIELDS ARE FULL

Edward Shanks

C. Armstrong Gibbs
(1889-1960)

Lento, dolcissimo ed espressivo

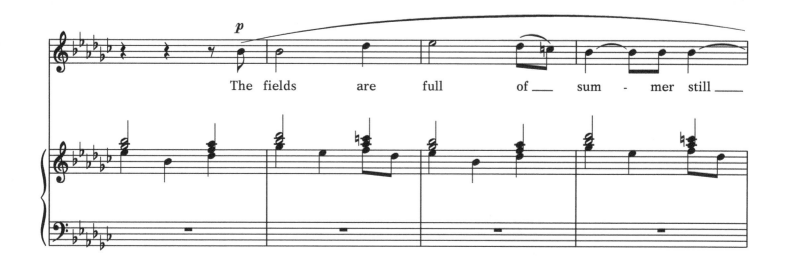

The fields are full of ___ sum - mer still ___

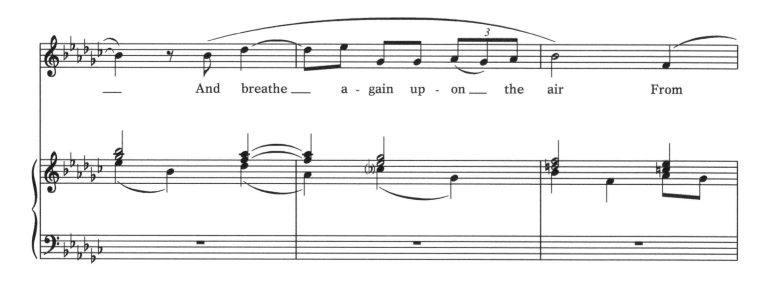

___ And breathe ___ a - gain up - on ___ the air   From

brown dry side ⎯⎯ of hedge and hill More

sweet - ness ⎯⎯ than the ⎯⎯ sense ⎯⎯ can bear.

So some old

cou - ple, who in youth With love ⎯⎯ were filled ⎯⎯

52

J'AI PLEURÉ EN RÊVE
(I wept, beloved, as I dreamed)

Gérard de Nerval
(after the German of Heinrich Heine)
English version by Carl Engel

Georges Hüe
(1858-1948)

J'ai pleu-ré en rê - ve;
I wept, be - lov - ed,

J'ai rê - vé que tu é - tais mor - te;
as I dreamed thou hadst gone to heav'n - ly spheres;

Je m'é-veil-lai,
And when I woke

et les lar - mes cou - lè - rent de mes jou - es.
there burst from mine eyes a burn-ing flood of tears.

J'ai pleu-ré en rê - ve; J'ai rê - vé que tu me quit-tais;
I wept, be - lov - ed, as I dreamed thou hadst for-sak-en me;

Je m'é-veil-lai, et je pleu-rai a-mè - re - ment long-temps a -
And when I woke I sobbed and cried all the gray morn, my love, for

près. J'ai pleu-ré en rê - ve; J'ai rê - vé
thee. I wept, be - lov - ed, as I dreamed

I MOURN AS A DOVE

from *St. Peter*

Julius Benedict
(1804-1885)

IL MIO BEN QUANDO VERRÀ

(When, my love, wilt thou return)

English version by Theodore Baker

Giovanni Paisiello
(1741-1816)

dol — ci, più dol — — ci ac — cen — — ti.
gen — — tly, more gen — — tly re — ply — — ing.

Ma non l'o — do.
Who can hear him?

E chi l'u — dì?
No voice hear I!

Ah! il mio be — ne am — mu — to — lì.
Ah! still my lov — er makes no re — ply.

Ah! am — mu — to — lì.
Ah! makes no re — ply.

Tu cui stan - ca o - ma - i già ____ fe'
Kind - ly ech - o, whose pa - tience with ____ me

il mio ____ pian - to, e - co ____ pie - to - sa,
My com - plain - ings al - read - y do ____ tire, ____

ei ri - tor - na e dol - ce a ____ te
Now re - turn ____ them, and gen - tly to thee

chie - - - de, chie - de ____ la ____ spo - - -
Draw ____ thou my ____ fond ____ de - sire. ____

THE LORD'S NAME IS PRAISED
(Praise the Lord ye servants)

Maurice Greene
(1696-1755)

down, ___ the go - ing ___ down of ___ the ___

same. The

Lord's _____ name _ is ___ prais - - -

- - - ed, from the

ris - - - - - - - - ing up of the sun, un-to the go - ing _ down _ of the _ same, un-to the go - ing down, the go - ing down _ of the same.

The Lord is high a - bove all hea - then,

the Lord is high a - bove all hea - then,

and his glo - ry a - bove the heav'ns,

and his glo - ry a - bove the heav'ns, ____

heav'ns, _____ his glo - -

ry a-bove the heav'ns, a-bove the heav'ns, a-bove the heav'ns.

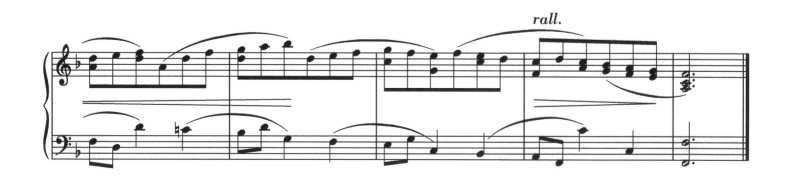

LOVE IS A PLAINTIVE SONG

from *Patience*

W.S. Gilbert

Arthur Sullivan
(1842-1900)

MANDOLINE

Paul Verlaine
English version by Marion Farquhar

Gabriel Fauré
(1845-1924)

Les don-neurs_____ de sé-ré-na_____-des
Gal-lants fond_____-ly ser-e-nad_____-ing

Et les bel_____-les é-cou-teu_____-ses   E-
And their la_____-dies all__ at ease,_____   Ex-

chan-gent des pro-pos fa — des, Sous les— ra-mu — — res chan — — ing
change ro-man-tic pat — ter, Be — neath the sing — — — ing

teu — — — — — — ses._____
trees. _____

Ped. *Ped.* *Ped.* *Ped.*

C'est Tir-cis _____ et c'est— A-min — — — te,
Here, Tir-cis*_____ and here,— A-min — — — te,+

Et c'est l'é-ter-nel Cli-tan-dre,_____ Et c'est Da-
And e-ter-nal Cli-tan-dra,_____ And there, Da-

*Tir-cees
+A-man-ta

78

* Da-mees

MAUSFALLEN-SPRÜCHLEIN
(The Mouser's Magic Verses)

Eduard Mörike

Hugo Wolf
(1860-1903)

verhallend

schein, Mon - den - schein! _____ Mach' a - ber die
bright, *moon- light* *night!* _____ *Close win- dow and*

Tür fein hin - ter dir zu, hörst du? hörst du?
door; on en- t'ring, my dear, d'you hear? d'you hear?

Da - bei hü - te dein Schwänz-chen! hörst du? hörst du? Dein
lest your tail get a nip - ping! d'you hear? d'you hear? A

Schwänz-chen!
nip - ping.

Nach Ti - sche sin - gen wir, nach
We'll feast till break of day, and

Ti - sche sprin - gen wir und ma - chen ein Tänz - chen, ___ ein Tänz - chen! _
sing a roun - da - lay, then gai - ly go trip - ping, ___ go trip - ping! _

rauh

Witt witt! Witt witt! mei - ne al - te Kat - ze tanzt wahr - schein - lich mit, hörst
Witt witt! Witt witt! Tab - by, my old cat, he'll dance, and you per - mit, d'you

du? hörst du? hörst du?
hear? d'you hear? d'you hear?

MONDNACHT
(Moonlight)

Joseph von Eichendorff
English version by Arthur Westbrook

Robert Schumann
(1810-1856)

Teneramente, misterioso (*Zart, heimlich*)

con Pedale

a tempo   *p*

Es war, als hätt' _____ der
It seem'd as tho' _____ the

Him - mel die Er - de still _____ ge -
heav - ens Had kiss'd the earth _____ to

küsst,   dass sie im Blü - then -
rest,   That she, 'mid moon - lit

wog - ten sacht;
wav - ing corn;
es rausch - ten
'Mid rus - tling

leis' _____ die Wäl - der;
for - est shad - ows
so stern - klar
The stars shone

war _____ die Nacht.
mild - ly on.
Und mei - ne
My soul with

See - le spann - te
out - spread pin - ions,
weit ih - re
Long - ing from

MY SWEETHEART AND I

Félix Bovet

Amy Beach
(1867-1944)

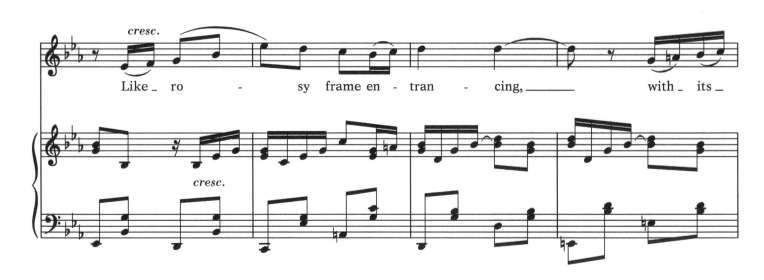

swal - low that _ her - alds the com - ing of

May _____

Like _ the _ fawn that _ doth _

fol - low the _ white _ flow - er _ al -

way, _____ Ah! _____

LE ROSSIGNOL DES LILAS
(The Nightingale and the Lilacs)

Léopold Dauphin
English version by Harry Goldby

Reynaldo Hahn
(1875-1947)

Modéré mais sans lenteur et avec élan

Ô pre-mier ros-si-gnol qui viens Dans les li-las, sous ma fe-
Oh the first night-in-gale to pass My win-dow, to see my

nê - tre, Ta voix___ m'est dou - ce à re-con-naî - tre! Nul ac-
li - lacs, Your song___ so sweet___ lets me re-mem - ber! No one's

cent n'est sem-bla - ble au tien!___
voice can re-sem - ble yours!___

Fi - dè - le aux a - mou - reux li - ens, _____ Trille en - cor   di - vin   pe - tit
And faith - ful to sweet bonds of love, _____ Trill once more,   di - vine   lit - tle

tendrement

ê - tre!   Ô   pre - mier   ros - si - gnol   qui viens   Dans
be - ing!   Oh   the first   night - in - gale   to   pass   My

les li - las, _____ sous ma fe - nê - tre!
win - dow, _____ to see my li - lacs!

dolce

un peu ralenti   *a tempo*

Noc - tur - ne ou ma - ti - nal _____ com -
By night _____ or in the morn - ing,   how

p suivez

sans rigueur

bien Ton hymne à l'a - mour ___ me pé - nê - tre! Tant d'ar-deur fait en
well Your hymn meant for love ___ pen- e-trates me! With such ar - dor I

cresc.

moi re - naî - tre L'é - cho de mes a - vrils an - ciens, ___
hear a - gain ___ The e - cho of my A - prils past, ___

espr.

chanté

à peine retardé

mf   p

opt.

Ô pre - mier ros - si - gnol qui viens! ___
O the first night- in- gale to come! ___

p suivez

p

NIEMAND HAT'S GESEH'N
(No One Saw at All)

Otto Friedrich Gruppe

Johann Karl Gottfried Loewe
(1796-1869)

102

NON TI FIDAR
(Don't be too sure!)
from *Muzio Scevola*

English version by Shibley Boyes

George Frideric Handel
(1685-1759)

Non ti fi -
Don't be too

dar, per - chè il de - si _ re lu - sin - ga _ è ver!
sure! Al - though de - sire's al - lur - ing, it's true,

mà poi so - ven - te A - mor è fal - so, fal - so,
rap - ture of _ love is of - ten fleet - ing, fleet - ing.

ven - te A - mo - re è fal - so, A - mo - re è fal - so, e il tem-po in -
love is of - ten fleet - ing, is of - ten fleet - ing. Pres - ent en -

gan - na, e il tem - po in - gan - - - - na,___ e il tem-po in -
chant - ment is mis - lead - - - - ing, joys of the

gan - na, in - gan - na, in - gan - na, e il tem-po in - gan - na,
mo - ment quick-ly pass, mis - lead - ing, joys of the mo - ment

in - gan - na.
quick-ly pass.

Chi vuol go - der, ho_in - te - so_a di - re, fis - sa_il pen - sier
He who'd en - joy life's full - est mea - sure, hear my ad - vice:

nel ben pre - sen - te: chè l'av - ve - ni - re ha_in man la sor - te
live for the pres - ent, be - ware the fu - ture, fate is in hid - ing,

cie - ca_e ti - ran - na, e ti - ran - na, cie - ca_e ti - ran - na.
blind and re - lent - less she ap - pears, blind and re - lent - less.

QUEL RUSCELLETTO
(The Brooklet)

Pietro Domenico Paradies
(1707-1791)

Where is the course of the brook-let lead - ing? 'Tis gai - ly speed-ing to __
Quel ru-scel-let - to Che l'on - de chia - re Or or col ma - re Con -

meet __ the sea, __ Spark-ling _ and foam-ing in rest - less roam - ing,
fon - de - rà, __ Nel mor-mo - ri - o Del fuo - co mi - o

SORRY HER LOT WHO LOVES TOO WELL

from *HMS Pinafore*

W.S. Gilbert

Arthur Sullivan
(1842-1900)

eyes ____ that speak too plain - ly. Sor - ry her lot ____ who

loves _ too well, Heav-y the heart that hopes but vain - ly.

rall.

Un poco animato

Heav - y the sor - row that bows ____ the head When love is a -

cresc.

live ____ and hope ____ is dead! When love is a - live and

f *dim.*

colla voce

hope _____ is dead!

Andante

Sad is the hour _____ when sets the sun— Dark is the

night _____ to earth's poor daugh - ters, When _____ to the ark _ the

wea - ried one Flies from the emp - ty waste of wa - ters.

SPRING

Thomas Nashe

Ivor Gurney
(1890-1937)

Spring, the sweet Spring, is the year's pleas-ant King, Then blooms each thing, then maids dance in a ring,

And we hear aye birds

tune this mer - ry lay— Cuc - koo,

jug - jug, pu - we, to - wit - ta - woo!

to Sara

SURE ON THIS SHINING NIGHT

James Agee*

Samuel Barber
(1910-1981)

*From "Permit Me Voyage". Used by permission of Yale University Press, Publishers.

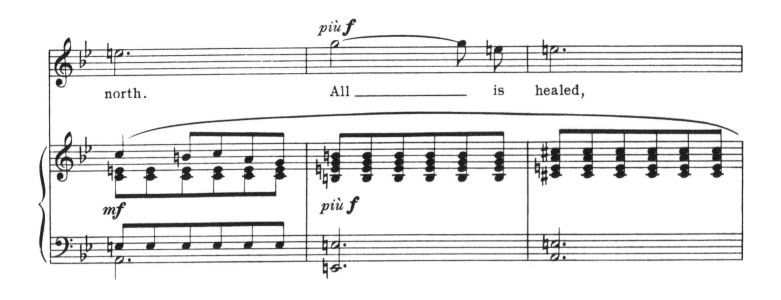

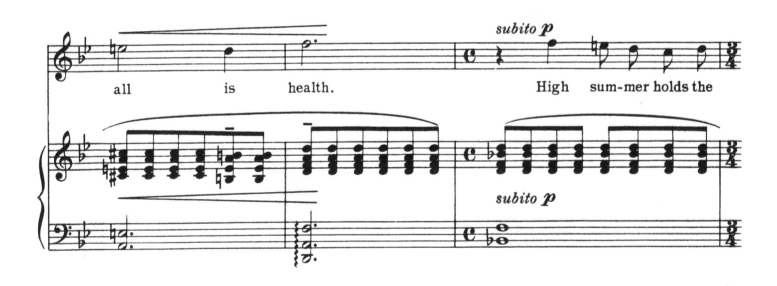

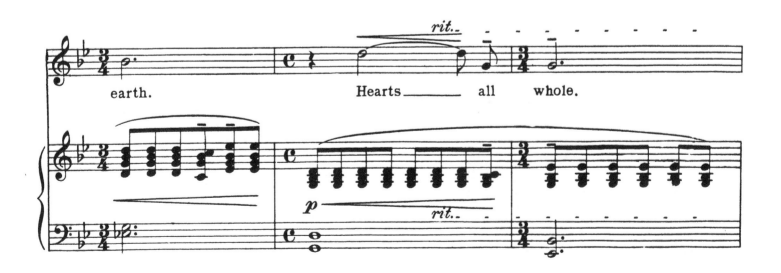

STÄNDCHEN
(Serenade)

Franz Kugler
English version by Florence Easton

Johannes Brahms
(1833-1897)

Anmuthig bewegt
Allegretto grazioso

Der Mond steht ü - ber dem Ber - ge, so recht für ver -
The moon hangs o - ver the hill - top, just right for young

lieb - te Leut'; im Gar - ten rie - selt ein
folks in love; The foun - tain mur - murs in the

THAT'S LIFE

Josephine Royle*

John P. Sacco

*Words used by permission.

Once I hoped that For-tune would be kind But she nev-er smiled on me —

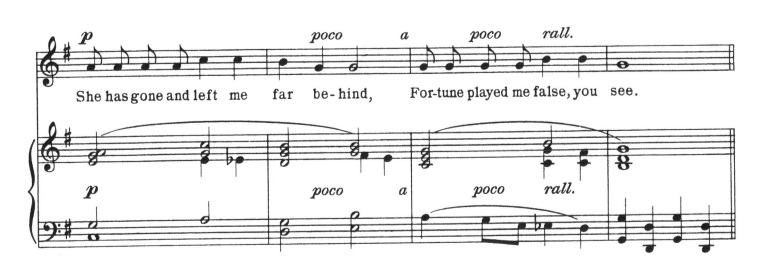

She has gone and left me far be-hind, For-tune played me false, you see.

poco   *a*   *poco*   *rall.*

Slower ♩= 72

Ev-'ry-thing that I do Al-ways seems to fall through— Why it is I can-not ex-

sane, ____ For I had found, in dis-may, E-ven love can be-tray— That's

Faster ♩= 116

life and it's so use-less to com - plain! Please tell me what life is all a-

bout, ____ I can't find out. Please tell me what love is all a-

WIND

Leonard Feeney

Theodore Chanler
(1902-1961)

Wind is to show How a thing can blow, _____

And es-pe-cial-ly through

trees; _____ When it is fast It is called a blast,

Words used by exclusive permission.

And re-turns to a sigh_____ once more.

Wind is the air In your hair,_____ When you stand On the sand By the

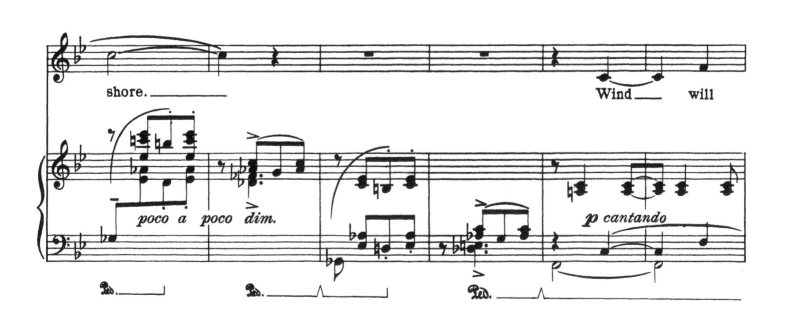

shore._____ Wind____ will

poco a poco dim. *p cantando*

shake the lat-tic-es late at night, It will

make the clouds go by; An-y-thing eas-y that's

hard to do, It is pret-ty sure to try:

THINK ON THESE THINGS

Adapted from
Philippians 4:4-8

June Caldwell Kirlin
(b. 1910)

Moderato, espressivo

What-so-ev-er things are beau-ti-ful, so beau-ti-ful, think on these things. What-so-ev-er things are hon-est and

true and love - ly, think on these things. If there

be an - y vir - tue, if there be an - y praise, re -

joice, re - joice in the Lord.

Think __ on these __ things, think on these things. Be

beau - ti - ful, so beau - ti - ful, think on these

things. What - so - ev - er things are hon - est and true and

love - ly, think on these things. These things do and peace

un - to you, peace un - to you.

TO ONE WHO PASSED WHISTLING THROUGH THE NIGHT

Margery Agrell

C. Armstrong Gibbs
(1889-1960)

Some - thing hath called me, Called me from far dreams. _____ The nak - ed trees are quiv - er - ing with de - light.

Do dreams still __ hold me, That faint mu - sic

streams A-cross the haunt - ed si - lence ____ of the

loco

night?

Won - der hath ris - en,

fair   The tide   of   sil - ver   mu - sic _____   ebbs   and

flows. _____

(one breath)

Ah _____

THE WHITE PEACE

Fiona Macleod

Arnold Bax
(1883-1953)